Ann Hayes

# PATCH PICTURES

## A Creative Guide to Fabric Collage

This book is dedicated, with love, to
*Oubie, for his love and patience*
*Yvette, for her praise and encouragement*
*Mauritz, for his laughter and criticism*

# PATCH PICTURES

## A Creative Guide to Fabric Collage

### NORMA SLABBERT

*Illustrations by Stephan Thelmore*
*Photographs by Peter Bouman*

NEW
HOLLAND

First published in the UK in 1988 by
New Holland (Publishers) Ltd
37 Connaught Street, London W2 2AZ

*Editor:* Jan Schaafsma
*Designer:* Janice Evans

Typeset by Diatype Setting cc
Reproduction by Photo Sepro (Pty) Ltd
Printed and bound by CTP Book Printers
BD8182

# CONTENTS

# Introduction

This book describes how to make pictures by gluing together pieces of fabric: this is called fabric or cloth collage. The word collage is derived from the French word "coller", which means "to glue". It is an exciting, unrestricted art form which does not require any particular artistic talent or skill.

Now that art and technology have become sophisticated and almost inaccessible there is a nostalgic tendency to return to the more traditional art forms such as appliqué, which is within everyone's capabilities. Not everyone is fortunate enough to have a sewing machine to make appliqué pictures, nor is everyone equally handy at using one. If you are one of these people, but have always wanted to make pictures using material, fabric collage is the answer.

Fortunately we live in times in which there is a strong emphasis on experimentation, and it is for this reason that fabric collage is so fascinating. It is an enchanting experience in which there is no right or wrong — only limitless possibilities. I like to call it a "compromise" art form, because you do not have to be an artist or be proficient in needlework to experience the joy of fabric and colour. The ability to select fabric of the right colour and texture for a particular picture is acquired gradually, as is the ability to reduce realistic things to their basic forms.

*Norma Slabbert*

*In this happy harvest festival scene it is the movement and use of colour that one especially notices. Strips of fabric with different printed patterns suggest the harvested fields.*

We all have a need to express ourselves creatively and the importance of this need should never be underestimated. Unfortunately many people never satisfy this need because they say, "I can't draw." But a pair of scissors can often be more sympathetic than a pencil and paper.

Fabric has a great advantage over other artistic media in that the colours and textures are ready-made: cutting a few pieces of brightly coloured material into interesting shapes is a simple matter. It is inexpensive and readily available, as every home usually has a wealth of old fabric. The composition of a picture, too, is easier using fabric because the cut-out shapes can be moved about freely on the background material until you have a satisfactory composition. When a particular colour does not look right, it can easily be replaced by a piece of material of another colour. Fabric can be manipulated. It can be crumpled and creased, folded and frayed, shrunk and stretched, pleated and pasted. Fabric can be stitched and creatively decorated with embroidery stitches.

A voyage of discovery through a new world awaits you once you begin experimenting with fabric. With a pair of scissors, pieces of material and glue, you can depict your ideals, dreams, memories and fantasies. Initially you may tend to copy existing designs, but as you become more confident about design, technique, colour and cloth you may feel the desire to create pictures that reflect your individuality. The approach of this book is therefore not prescriptive: it is, rather, an attempt to inspire you.

For this reason the work of a few other fabric artists has been included. Each explains her approach to fabric art, what inspires her, and her method of working. Their work is strikingly different but they do have one thing in common − pleasure in their creation and a love of fabric. This is inspiring and it will give you a broader view and an open mind regarding the world of fabric, colour and texture.

Before you begin to do a picture, I would like to give you some background information on the potential of fabric, the choice of a subject, and basic equipment and techniques; this will give you more self-confidence when tackling your first picture.

# CHAPTER 1
## *What can I do?*

Almost every artist begins with the question: What can I do? The answer is simple: look around you! There are so many possibilities it can be bewildering.

Art lies in the way you look at things. You should learn to look at things with an eye that identifies and isolates the main element. Perhaps when looking out of the window you see a group of guinea fowl running across the lawn: they dodge nervously through the long grass when a red car drives past. A dog chases the car but decides it is easier to chase his tail. This he does without further ado among the ranunculuses, which are a riot of colour but at the moment are hanging their heads in the rain.

This could be the theme of a cheerful, colourful picture, but it could also result in utter confusion. Learn to isolate the things that really interest you. What was it that really attracted your attention? The frightened scurrying of the guinea fowl, the antics of the dog, or the ranunculuses hanging their heads? When I had to choose from all these impressions I was struck most by the alarm and watchfulness of the guinea fowl, and I tried to portray this.

It takes time, practice and many mistakes to learn to observe and portray only the essential details. A good exercise is to look at a landscape or subject through an empty frame. You can eliminate more detail by looking at the world around you through a piece of paper made into a tube. (Do this in the city and watch people's reactions!)

Where do you find inspiration? Some ideas:
- Always keep a sketchbook handy.
- Make notes of what interests or excites you, and rough sketches of your ideas.
- Together with these ideas, note details such as colour, texture and shapes that may form a pattern.
- Think of suitable pieces of fabric while you are collecting ideas.
- While you are walking in town, for example, take note of the shapes of buildings. What shapes are the windows? What colours are the buildings? How many shades of grey do you see? What bricks have been used? Look analytically.
- Look at the way people sit, stand, play, run, move, fight, gossip or sleep. Do not be afraid of using people in your pictures. They make a place less lonely. Think of the spontaneous naïve figures that children like to draw.
- Take photographs during an outing in

natural surroundings. Try to remember what attracted your attention the most, but portray only the essentials. Collage requires a degree of simplification which is possible only if you distance yourself from the environment. Try to convey the feel of the landscape.

☐ Get yourself a file in which to keep your good ideas. These could be photographs, brochures, advertisements, cartoons or illustrations from newspapers or magazines. Line drawings in advertisements will give you a good idea of how an artist simplifies a subject. Pictures with a particularly striking use of colour and colour combinations are good sources of inspiration, particularly if you have not yet developed an instinct for colour yourself. Use these pictures as inspiration only, because it is far easier to make an original picture than to try to copy one.

☐ Choose a subject in which you are genuinely interested, not one simply for its graphic quality. Try to convey your own feelings about it.

☐ Sometimes you reach a stage at which you really do not know what to do. First of all, enjoy a few days' rest. Refill your memory bank with impressions and inspiration from external things. Visit art exhibitions, museums, galleries, an aviary, flower shows, fabric shops or your local library. A new idea may strike you and grow, and you will gradually develop your own style.

☐ Analyse the work of other artists. Look at their subjects, their detail and their use of colour. Look at the way collage has been practised as folk art of one kind or another for years. Look at the work of pioneers such as Picasso, Braque, Matisse or Klee. The naïve forest scenes of Henri Rousseau may inspire you to use all the shades of green material lying crumpled up in the cupboard.

☐ Fabric collage allows you to escape into a fantasy world. In this way you can observe the lighter side of the world in which you live and depict it naïvely and colourfully in fabric. A bundle of dirty washing is no fun, but in a colourful collage it is pure pleasure and provides a great deal of satisfaction. Not all of us live in a world that is as pretty as a picture. It is at times like these that you have to look for small details that are beautiful and inspiring. A dirty and unplastered brick wall is rich in texture and can be full of character.

☐ Humour occurs naturally in collage. Write down everything that makes you laugh or feel light-hearted. Anything that is cheerful and rich in colour will make an excellent subject. Think of balloons, umbrellas or someone standing on a chair and shrieking at the sight of a mouse.

☐ Family photographs are probably the most interesting source of inspiration. The picture opposite was inspired by such a look at old photo-albums. While we were all

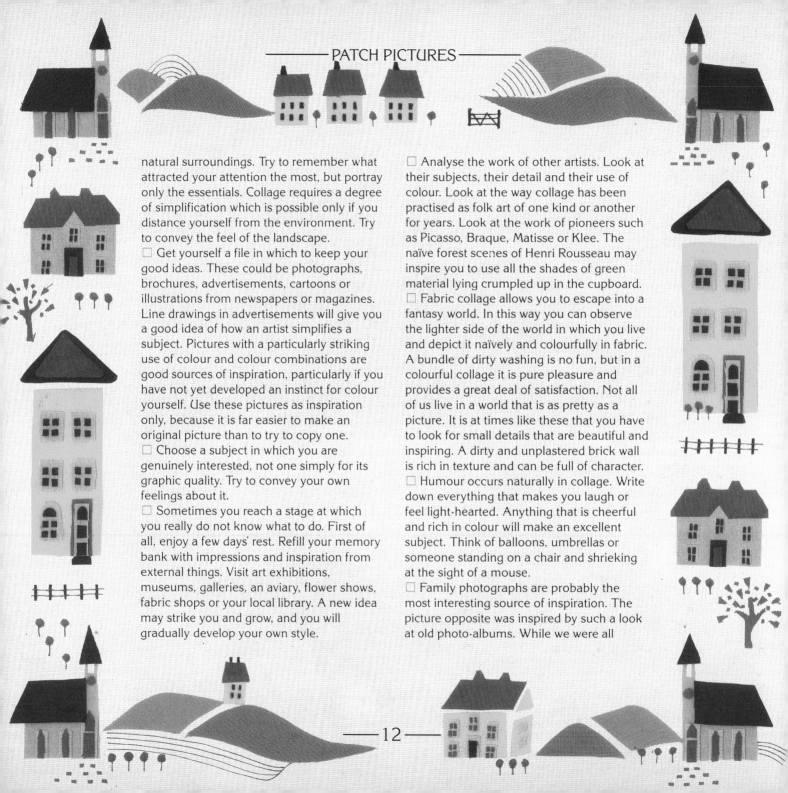

*The inspiration for a fabric collage can come from anywhere. The basis for this picture was laid when the family paged through old photo-albums.*

*This picture was the result of an accident. The child who had made the original dropped it in a puddle. After her tears were dried, it was decided to preserve the picture for posterity by making this collage.*

having a good laugh, the idea came to me to make a "do you remember" picture for a child's room. The background material was cut to resemble a number of photographs, and then it was easy to portray the things that were important to each member of the family. It included the sunflowers we sowed each year, the old-fashioned pram that embarrassed everybody, all our pets, the ducks who paddled about in the pool, the weal and woe of the two birds who chose to nest in the birdbath, and the bunch of flowers with which it all started . . . What about a picture of a wedding with the emphasis on the ugliest hat of the day? A baptism, a birthday party, the family home, cat or vacation are all good subjects. Pictures such as these can take on a very personal note, for example by using material from old clothes.

☐ Your sewing cupboard can be a source of great inspiration. The pattern, colour and texture of a piece of fabric often determine what you are going to make. As you know, a piece of blue and white striped material looks like a butcher's apron, and yellow and red stripes might remind you of a circus tent. Small white dots on dark blue could be guinea fowl. An old floral green and violet coloured silk blouse could be transformed into mysterious forest flowers.

☐ Inspiration sometimes comes from unexpected sources. A child runs home one afternoon after school, full of excitement, to share her painting with her mother. She slips and falls in a puddle of water which, together with her tears, almost ruins the picture. A sympathetic mother, a few pieces of fabric and some glue save the situation.

☐ Pictures do not have to be realistic. You can experiment with abstract art where colour, line, texture, shape and pattern become more important than a pretty picture. Look for inspiration in nature or in some form of natural life. Think of the scales of a fish, pebbles on a beach, a tree trunk or melon seeds. The list is endless.

# CHAPTER 2

# *The potential of fabric*

Half the joy in every picture lies in choosing the pieces of material. A picture begins to take shape the moment you start to think of or look for the right fabric to express an idea. The best way of getting to know fabric is to handle as much of it as possible. Almost any kind of fabric is suitable for collage. Experiment with it. See how various fabrics react to being glued, cut, frayed, unravelled and torn.

## CHOOSING MATERIAL

Build up a large collection of fabrics of different colours. Beg, borrow or steal from friends and dressmakers. Rummage around at street markets or jumble sales. The fabric of old items of clothing has a patina that is full of character. Ask your friends for their old clothes, napkins, tablecloths, curtains, scarves and ties. Advertise your needs and you will see how much fabric finds its way to you. Collect pieces of material in a variety of textures and patterns. Geometric patterns such as dots, stripes and checks have a timeless, abstract quality that gives texture to a picture.

Small designs are charming, but also collect pieces of material with large flowing patterns such as paisley, or exotic batik designs. Cut into small pieces, these give life and movement to a picture. They can also tone down a picture if it is too busy because too many pieces of fabric with small designs have been used. However, be careful with fabric which threatens to dominate a picture.

Fabric that does not fray or unravel is easy to work with and is well-suited to collage, but loosely woven fabric that frays and unravels easily is also essential. A rooster's feathers look better if they are a little frayed at the edges.

Collect fabrics and pieces of material that you like. Ten pieces of ugly material are not suddenly going to become beautiful when they are used in a picture! Be careful, however, not to become stereotyped in this way in your choice of fabrics. Also try to use unusual fabrics that would possibly not be your first choice but which have interesting possibilities.

## BACKGROUND FABRIC

Choose a firm, good-quality fabric for the background. This will be glued onto a piece of cardboard. Plain fabric is usually the most suitable but some curtain or upholstery fabric,

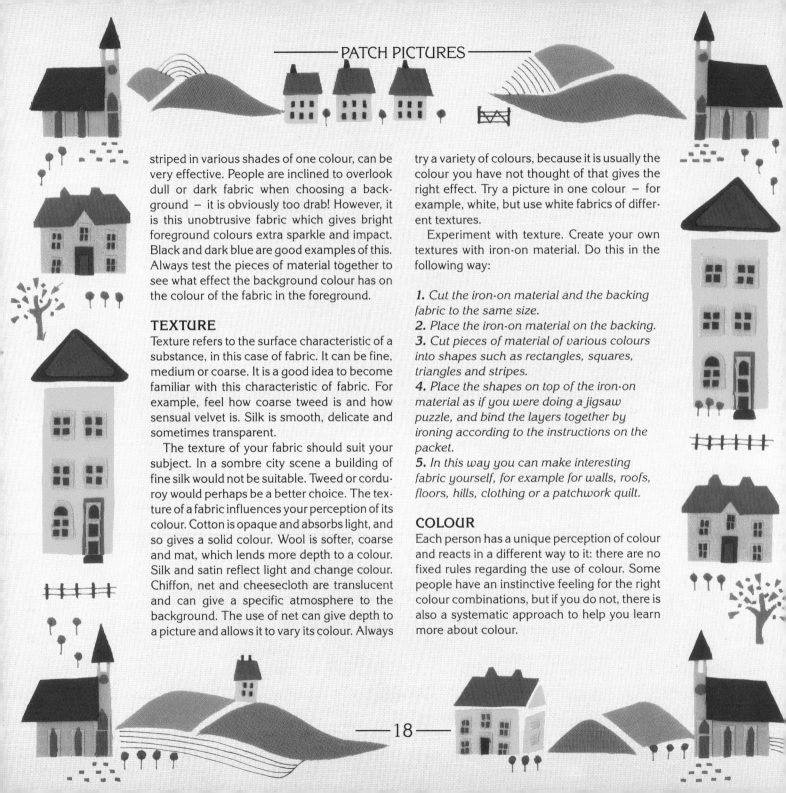

striped in various shades of one colour, can be very effective. People are inclined to overlook dull or dark fabric when choosing a background – it is obviously too drab! However, it is this unobtrusive fabric which gives bright foreground colours extra sparkle and impact. Black and dark blue are good examples of this. Always test the pieces of material together to see what effect the background colour has on the colour of the fabric in the foreground.

## TEXTURE

Texture refers to the surface characteristic of a substance, in this case of fabric. It can be fine, medium or coarse. It is a good idea to become familiar with this characteristic of fabric. For example, feel how coarse tweed is and how sensual velvet is. Silk is smooth, delicate and sometimes transparent.

The texture of your fabric should suit your subject. In a sombre city scene a building of fine silk would not be suitable. Tweed or corduroy would perhaps be a better choice. The texture of a fabric influences your perception of its colour. Cotton is opaque and absorbs light, and so gives a solid colour. Wool is softer, coarse and mat, which lends more depth to a colour. Silk and satin reflect light and change colour. Chiffon, net and cheesecloth are translucent and can give a specific atmosphere to the background. The use of net can give depth to a picture and allows it to vary its colour. Always

try a variety of colours, because it is usually the colour you have not thought of that gives the right effect. Try a picture in one colour – for example, white, but use white fabrics of different textures.

Experiment with texture. Create your own textures with iron-on material. Do this in the following way:

*1.* *Cut the iron-on material and the backing fabric to the same size.*
*2.* *Place the iron-on material on the backing.*
*3.* *Cut pieces of material of various colours into shapes such as rectangles, squares, triangles and stripes.*
*4.* *Place the shapes on top of the iron-on material as if you were doing a jigsaw puzzle, and bind the layers together by ironing according to the instructions on the packet.*
*5.* *In this way you can make interesting fabric yourself, for example for walls, roofs, floors, hills, clothing or a patchwork quilt.*

## COLOUR

Each person has a unique perception of colour and reacts in a different way to it: there are no fixed rules regarding the use of colour. Some people have an instinctive feeling for the right colour combinations, but if you do not, there is also a systematic approach to help you learn more about colour.

# THE POTENTIAL OF FABRIC

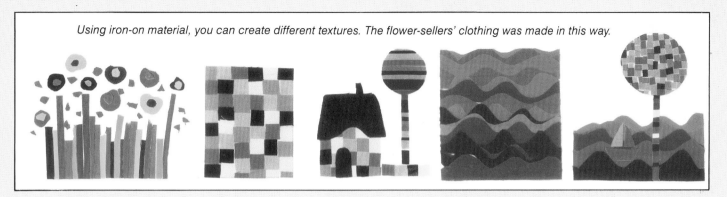

*Using iron-on material, you can create different textures. The flower-sellers' clothing was made in this way.*

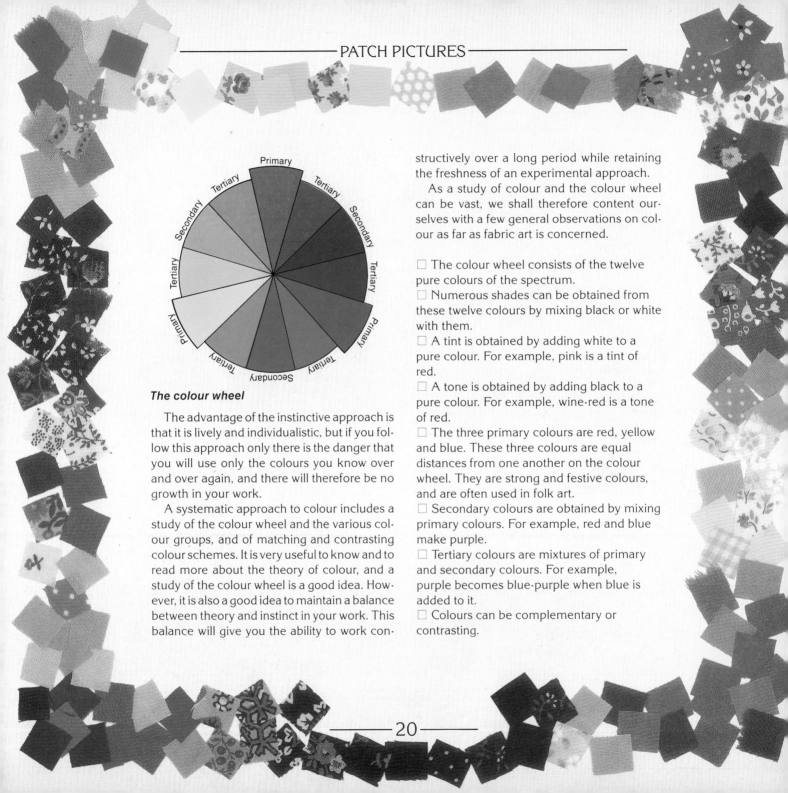

**The colour wheel**

The advantage of the instinctive approach is that it is lively and individualistic, but if you follow this approach only there is the danger that you will use only the colours you know over and over again, and there will therefore be no growth in your work.

A systematic approach to colour includes a study of the colour wheel and the various colour groups, and of matching and contrasting colour schemes. It is very useful to know and to read more about the theory of colour, and a study of the colour wheel is a good idea. However, it is also a good idea to maintain a balance between theory and instinct in your work. This balance will give you the ability to work con-structively over a long period while retaining the freshness of an experimental approach.

As a study of colour and the colour wheel can be vast, we shall therefore content our-selves with a few general observations on col-our as far as fabric art is concerned.

☐ The colour wheel consists of the twelve pure colours of the spectrum.

☐ Numerous shades can be obtained from these twelve colours by mixing black or white with them.

☐ A tint is obtained by adding white to a pure colour. For example, pink is a tint of red.

☐ A tone is obtained by adding black to a pure colour. For example, wine-red is a tone of red.

☐ The three primary colours are red, yellow and blue. These three colours are equal distances from one another on the colour wheel. They are strong and festive colours, and are often used in folk art.

☐ Secondary colours are obtained by mixing primary colours. For example, red and blue make purple.

☐ Tertiary colours are mixtures of primary and secondary colours. For example, purple becomes blue-purple when blue is added to it.

☐ Colours can be complementary or contrasting.

*Texture can make a big difference to a picture. The feathers simply look better if they are frayed a bit.*

*My most precious possession is this friendship collage made from begged fabric and neckties. My lady friends each supplied a piece of cloth from an old item of clothing, and the gentlemen their old ties. Of all my pictures, this has been the most fun.*

☐ Single colours are used in monochromatic colour schemes. They are the differing values and intensities of one colour, for example, from light blue to dark blue. This could be monotonous, but if the shades vary from light to dark, or from bright to dull, and if different patterns in blue such as checks, stripes, dots or fine florals are used, a colour scheme of this type can be interesting.

A related colour scheme uses analogous colours. This is to use two or three colours next to or close to one another on the colour wheel.

Pure colours next to one another may be too harsh. Instead, you could use tints and tones of these colours. Shades of pink and light orange are softer than red and orange.

☐ Complementary colours are exactly opposite one another on the colour wheel, for example, blue and orange, yellow and purple, and red and green. These colours are not usually used in the same quantities. Using even the smallest amount of a complementary colour is enough to add sparkle to a picture. The intensity of these colours can also be reduced.

☐ White and black also have a place in fabric art. White can create a strong contrast or make colours stand out, whereas black can add mystery and depth to a picture.

☐ The neutral colours are those of sand, brick, wood, stone, straw, ice and shells. These are good background colours.

☐ Colours can be warm or cool. Red, yellow and orange are warm colours and tend to move to the forefront. Blue, green, blue-green and blue-purple are cool colours and tend to remain in the background.

☐ Colour arouses specific emotions and is often used to create a particular atmosphere. For example, red says: "Look at me!" It is strong, challenging, active and stimulating, and too much of it can be aggressive.

☐ Yellow is sunny, cheerful and stimulating: it is the brightest of the primary colours. When using yellow, a good principle to follow is "a little goes a long way".

☐ Green is peaceful. It is the colour of life and decay in nature. Think of the difference in colour between young spring leaves and leaves that have been lying on the ground for a long time.

☐ Purple is luxurious, regal and elegant.

☐ Blue is calm, relaxed and passive.

☐ Brown combined with other colours is warm and friendly, but too much brown can be sombre and monotonous.

☐ Culture influences our feelings about colour. In the East white is worn for mourning. In the Catholic Church green is the colour of hope.

☐ Colours influence one another, and the only way to acquire more knowledge on this subject is to experiment.

Read more about colour and expand your

knowledge of it, but don't allow yourself to be restricted by this knowledge. Here are a few practical hints in connection with colour in fabric art:

☐ It is sometimes worthwhile to forget your own colour preferences and build up a large colour palette.

☐ Collect as many shades of one colour as possible. Arrange your fabric according to colour values. Look at the colours with half-closed eyes. Pin the piece of fabric onto a noticeboard or hold it in front of a mirror. This will give you a better idea of colour intensity, depth and contrast. Look for printed fabrics where the complementary colours, for example, are brought together.

☐ Keep on experimenting with your fabrics. Be flexible. Let's say you are working on a picture and have decided on, for example, blue for a certain area. Before you glue the fabric down, try a few different shades of blue as well as other colours that might be suitable. You will be amazed at the way colour can change the atmosphere of a picture.

☐ Try a surprising colour, and a colour that does not immediately seem right. In a picture in which brown and cream dominate, pink can be interesting because it is unexpected.

☐ In a blue picture, green could be successful. In a cream picture red is unexpected, as is yellow in a black and grey picture. You could also mix cold and warm colours, for example, blue and orange.

☐ Experiment also with gold and silver fabric.

☐ Become more colour conscious. Take note of the use of colour in advertisements, magazines and paintings, and take particular note of colour in nature. Learn from colour combinations in nature.

☐ Our Creator is the greatest colourist. Think of the rainbow, a bird's feathers, a butterfly's wings. See how brilliant the adjacent colours of red, orange and yellow look in a bed of nasturtiums. Look at the contrasts in a bunch of ranunculuses: among the red, orange-red, pink, magenta and purple ranunculuses there is a colour that is perfectly complementary, and that is yellow.

☐ Think of a mood you could create using colour, for example, hot, cold, exciting, busy, dark, frightening or mysterious.

☐ Light plays an important part as far as colour is concerned. Look at the fabric you have selected for a particular picture in daylight as well as at night. Bear in mind also where the picture will be hanging. Bright colours can sometimes be too bright.

☐ If fabric of a specific colour continues to elude you, it is possible to dye or bleach fabric.

☐ Do not use too many colours in one

picture. Strangely enough this can make the picture look quite colourless or lifeless. Using a few colours in different shades and textures is more subtle, and the result is richer.

☐ If you want to do a cheerful, colourful picture, use mainly bright colours, but combine these with a few dark colours, too.

☐ Think of your fabric in the same way that you think of your friends: each one has his or her own personality. Some are richly coloured, sparkling, flamboyant, noisy, exciting, challenging, untidy, egotistical or always seeking attention. Others are calm, peaceful, neat, dull and uninteresting, but you can depend on them. A good mixture of these friends ensures a successful party. Friends who do not get on are not invited together, but those with completely different characters are, so that the conversation will be interesting and absorbing. Certain friends complement one another. Dull friends become more lively in the presence of colourful friends, and colourful friends become more dignified in a tranquil atmosphere. The colours for your picture should be chosen on the same basis.

## DESIGN

In these times of uniformity the spontaneous personal approach is still the most appealing. Some of the most beautiful fabric art work has been done by people who are not artists in the true sense of the word, and who have not had any artistic training or experience. These people have a sincere, spontaneous approach to colour, patterns, texture and design.

☐ Design includes the choice of a subject, or the simplification and arrangement of a collection of visual impressions.

☐ Design also involves line, shape and pattern. Lines can be straight, broad, narrow, close to or far from one another. They suggest direction, movement or stability. Shapes are formed when lines meet.

☐ Try not to give shapes subjective meanings immediately. Instead of thinking of, for example, the shapes of fish or of houses, think of shapes as expressions of movement. Think, for example, of shapes suggesting stability, peace or turbulence.

In fabric collage you will often be using off-cuts of various shapes. Look at these random shapes carefully, because they can be very useful and interesting. Shapes that are repeated form a pattern and, together with line, texture and colour, they form part of a design. Take the following points into account in your design and composition:

*1. Decide on the size of your picture.*
*2. Cut out four long strips of paper to make a "frame" within which to work.*

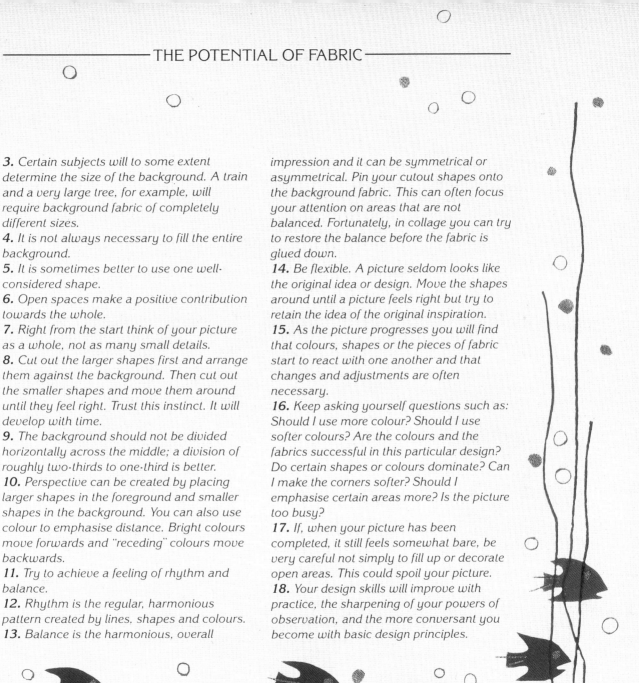

**3.** Certain subjects will to some extent determine the size of the background. A train and a very large tree, for example, will require background fabric of completely different sizes.

**4.** It is not always necessary to fill the entire background.

**5.** It is sometimes better to use one well-considered shape.

**6.** Open spaces make a positive contribution towards the whole.

**7.** Right from the start think of your picture as a whole, not as many small details.

**8.** Cut out the larger shapes first and arrange them against the background. Then cut out the smaller shapes and move them around until they feel right. Trust this instinct. It will develop with time.

**9.** The background should not be divided horizontally across the middle; a division of roughly two-thirds to one-third is better.

**10.** Perspective can be created by placing larger shapes in the foreground and smaller shapes in the background. You can also use colour to emphasise distance. Bright colours move forwards and "receding" colours move backwards.

**11.** Try to achieve a feeling of rhythm and balance.

**12.** Rhythm is the regular, harmonious pattern created by lines, shapes and colours.

**13.** Balance is the harmonious, overall impression and it can be symmetrical or asymmetrical. Pin your cutout shapes onto the background fabric. This can often focus your attention on areas that are not balanced. Fortunately, in collage you can try to restore the balance before the fabric is glued down.

**14.** Be flexible. A picture seldom looks like the original idea or design. Move the shapes around until a picture feels right but try to retain the idea of the original inspiration.

**15.** As the picture progresses you will find that colours, shapes or the pieces of fabric start to react with one another and that changes and adjustments are often necessary.

**16.** Keep asking yourself questions such as: Should I use more colour? Should I use softer colours? Are the colours and the fabrics successful in this particular design? Do certain shapes or colours dominate? Can I make the corners softer? Should I emphasise certain areas more? Is the picture too busy?

**17.** If, when your picture has been completed, it still feels somewhat bare, be very careful not simply to fill up or decorate open areas. This could spoil your picture.

**18.** Your design skills will improve with practice, the sharpening of your powers of observation, and the more conversant you become with basic design principles.

1. *Thread* 2. *Prestik* 3. *Pencil* 4. *Ruler* 5. *Ponal* 6. *Pritt Project Glue* 7. *Dressmaking scissors* 8. *Eraser* 9. *Colour pencils* 10. *Embroidery thread* 11. *General purpose scissors* 12. *Toothpicks* 13. *Craft scissors* 14. *Pins* 15. *Needlework scissors* 16. *Toothpicks with Prestik* 17. *Brush* 18. *Fabric* 19. *Iron-on material* 20. *Brown paper* 21. *Frame* 22. *Mount* 23. *Tracing paper*

# CHAPTER 3

# *Basic requirements*

One's requirements for making fabric pictures are few, and do not cost a great deal. Apart from the fabric, one needs scissors, cardboard and glue, as well as a few articles one probably has at home anyway.

## SORTING AND STORING

Nothing can dampen one's enthusiasm more effectively than a mountain of crumpled fabric that causes an avalanche every time the cupboard door is opened. It is necessary to maintain some order in your fabric collection; otherwise you will waste valuable time whenever you have to look for a particular piece of fabric. How you go about this will depend on your personal preferences or on the amount of space you have available. You can store fabric in shoeboxes, shirt boxes or plastic bags. A good idea is to sort the pieces according to colour or pattern, for example, or to store fabric of different designs, colours and brightness together. Fabric that has been ironed is easier to work with and takes up less space.

Fabric is so beautiful it is a pity to put it away in a cupboard. It is sheer pleasure to see and to feel all one's pieces of fabric every day. The colours simply make one feel lighthearted. After many uninspiring days I have found the ideal solution: take a few trouser hangers, iron your pieces of fabric, fold them into long strips, sort them according to colour and pattern, and hang them neatly over the hangers. Each piece of fabric shows a little of its colour and character – just enough to stimulate the imagination. This could form an inspiring colour collage against the wall above your work table. If you are worried about attracting dust, you could hang the hangers in a cupboard. Small off-cuts can be stored according to colour in plastic packets.

## ESSENTIAL EQUIPMENT

### Scissors

A good, durable pair of scissors is an investment. Look for the following in choosing one: finish, cutting capability, design, what it is made of, the ease with which it works, and the way it feels in your hand. Fiskars have a range of scissors that satisfy all these requirements. They also have scissors for left-handed people.

The advantage of this range of scissors is that they don't have to be sharpened. The Scissor Tuner keeps the blades in good condition. The following four kinds of scissors in the Fiskars range are useful for collage:

*Dressmaking scissors*
This pair of scissors is designed to cut anything from silk to suede. It has a comfortable handle design and is useful for cutting out larger patterns and shapes such as background fabric.

*General purpose scissors*
These you would use for cutting out paper patterns, cardboard and brown paper.

*Needlework scissors*
This small pair of scissors is the most important piece of equipment in collage. With it you "paint" or draw. Because of its sharp point it is easy to cut the smallest piece of fabric for windows, leaves or eyes. It is a good idea to wear this pair on a string around your neck while you work. Valuable time is lost if you have to keep hunting among the pieces of fabric for your scissors.

*Craft scissors*
These are exactly the same size as the needlework scissors but the points have been rounded to make them safe for children to use. Parents often make the mistake of buying a cheap pair of scissors of inferior quality for children. A blunt pair of scissors frustrates the child, and dampens enthusiasm and the creative urge. These craft scissors are the very best available.

**Glue**
You will need two kinds of glue:

*Pritt Project Glue; Gloy Children's Glue*
This is a white, milky glue, ideal for gluing fabric.

*Ponal; Unibond PVA*
This is a wood and paper glue for gluing paper and picture frames.

**Cardboard for the background**
Stiff, white cardboard onto which fabric can be glued. It should be firm so the glue does not make it curl.

**Fabric**
A variety of fabrics in various colours, designs and textures.

**Pritt Tak or pins**
I use Pritt Tak rather than pins because the pieces of fabric are often too small for a pin.

**Toothpicks**
☐ You can pick up even the smallest piece of fabric using Pritt Tak on the point of a toothpick.
☐ Toothpicks can also be used to spread glue onto fabric.

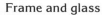

### Frame and glass

A completed fabric collage is safer behind glass because then the fabric does not fray or become soiled. It is also useful to use the glass to protect an unfinished picture while you are not working on it.

### An iron and ironing board

A steam iron is convenient but an ordinary iron will also do. Iron all fabric before cutting it.

## ADDITIONAL EQUIPMENT

The following items are not absolutely essential, but they are very useful:

☐ A file with a collection of inspiring ideas.
☐ A sketchbook, pencil, eraser and ruler.
☐ Brown paper, newsprint and a few old magazines for cutting out preliminary patterns.
☐ Tracing paper, if you want to make paper templates for your final design.
☐ A soft, clean paintbrush to clean the completed picture.
☐ Iron-on fabric which is fabric with either one or two adhesive surfaces. It joins fabric, and in certain instances is used instead of glue.
☐ Thread, which can be used to emphasise or outline certain areas. Fine details such as eyebrows, crows' feet, flower stems, water bubbles, and insects' feelers, etc, can be

done with thread. Collect a variety of colours and shades. Embroidery thread is also suitable. Metallic thread such as gold and silver can bring extra sparkle to a picture.

*Try a picture in one colour but use different textures, as in this abstract landscape by Cindy Bartos.*

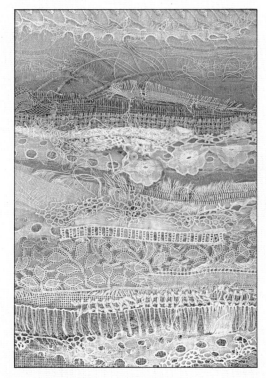

# CHAPTER 4

# Methods of working

In collage there are no fixed rules regarding a method of working. Your method will depend on your skill with a pair of scissors, glue and fabric. There are three basic methods to follow:

### Working from a sketch

☐ First make a rough sketch of your idea on paper.

☐ At the same time think of the colours and various kinds of fabric suitable for your design.

☐ The sketch will give you an idea of the size of your picture.

☐ Use the sketch only as a basic guideline. Fabric differs from paper and throughout the working process you will have to change details according to the colour and texture of the fabric.

☐ Initially you will possibly find it easier to make paper templates of your sketches and to work with those.

☐ With practice you will develop the self-confidence to cut the fabric into various shapes and to use the sketch only as a guide.

### Working with paper templates

☐ Make a preliminary sketch of your design. Now cut out paper templates according to your sketch.

☐ You can use tracing paper, but it is better to cut freehand. Even if the fabric does look a little uneven, it is spontaneous. This technique is eminently suited to fabric collage.

### The direct method

☐ With this method you use a pair of scissors in the same way as you would use a pencil: you "draw" with the scissors. This spontaneous method of working is probably the most suited to collage, but it requires thorough planning before you can start cutting.

### A few hints before you begin

*1. Decide more or less on the size of your picture, which could perhaps be determined by a frame you already have or by the position in which you want to hang the picture. I choose not to be restricted by the size of a frame.*

*2. Start with a picture that is not too large: you will then not give up as quickly!*
*3. Start with simple shapes.*
*4. If you already have a frame, bear in mind its colour when choosing the fabric. The frame forms an integral part of the picture and it is important for the colours of the fabric to harmonise with the frame. A good idea is to spread out the fabric and then to place the frame on top of it. See whether it feels and looks right.*
*5. If you have never made a fabric collage before and are a little hesitant about experimenting with expensive fabric, try the following exercise using paper. In itself it is a very satisfying, creative activity, and it will give you a good idea of the colour you will eventually be using in your fabric picture.*

This is what you do:

☐ Every picture starts with an idea.
☐ You could make a rough sketch of this idea but because you will be working with paper you could try cutting freehand.
☐ Look through old magazines and take note of the colour combinations and textures of various illustrations.
☐ Tear out illustrations with more or less the same colours that you intend using in your fabric picture.
☐ Use this coloured paper to cut out

templates for your picture, and using paper glue, glue them onto a cardboard background which should be the same size as your intended fabric picture. What you are now doing is paper collage.
☐ The paper product will give you a rough idea of what your fabric collage will look like in colour. You will, however, have to make further adjustments when you repeat the process using fabric, because the colour and texture of the paper differ from the colour and texture of fabric. Always be flexible.

## A FIRST PICTURE STEP BY STEP
Let's go through the steps for making your first picture. I suggest that this time you copy and use the template method in order to become familiar with the techniques of cutting out and gluing.

There are four different pictures, using one basic pattern, so you can experiment with various techniques such as cutting out and gluing, fraying the fabric, colour selection, gluing thread, working with iron-on fabric, and using stitching. Let us begin:

### Example 1
*1. Decide on a subject. In this case it is a house and tree, which is a simple and easy first subject.*
*2. Cut out a piece of firm background cardboard 17.5 x 12.5 cm for your picture.*

**Above:** *Sketch each picture roughly on paper. You could also colour it in.*
**Above right:** *Cut paper patterns from your sketch and move them around to achieve the right composition.*
**Right:** *Cut the patterns out of the fabric of your choice when you are satisfied with the design.*

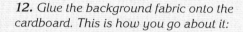

Also cut out a piece of sketching paper of the same size.

**3.** Make a rough sketch of the picture on the sketching paper. This time you can trace it (but do not tell your friends).

**4.** Now cut out paper templates from your sketch.

**5.** Put several small pieces of Pritt Tak on the back of each template.

**6.** Decide which pieces of material you are going to use for the foreground and which for the background.

**7.** Check to see what the foreground fabric looks like against the background fabric. Ask yourself the following questions: do the colours look good together? Does the colour of the background bring out the best in the foreground colours?

**8.** If you feel unsure about the correct choice of colour, you can use a piece of multi-coloured fabric to start with. In Example-1, I started off by putting the multi-coloured fabric on the foreground and tried to repeat the colours in it.

**9.** If you already have a frame, place it over the fabric you have selected. The frame forms an integral part of the picture so these two colours should go well together.

**10.** Iron all your fabric and lay it flat on your worktable.

**11.** Cut your background fabric to the same size as the cardboard (17.5 x 12.5 cm).

**12.** Glue the background fabric onto the cardboard. This is how you go about it:

☐ Spread Pritt Project Glue or Gloy Children's Glue over the cardboard.

☐ Using your finger or a strip of cardboard, spread it evenly over the whole surface, in the same way that you would spread butter on bread.

☐ Now place the background fabric lightly on the sticky surface of the cardboard.

☐ Rub lightly and quickly from the middle of the fabric outwards with your clean fingertips. The fabric is now stuck to the cardboard and you must try to iron out all bubbles or wrinkles with your fingers.

☐ Look out specifically for the following:

• Make sure that the whole surface of the cardboard is covered by glue, otherwise the fabric will bubble in the places where there is no glue.

• If there is too much glue on the cardboard it will come through onto the fabric. This is always a pity, but it is also an opportunity for problem-solving. Plant (or glue, rather!) a tree or a flower over the glue mark. A cloud, insect, fly or butterfly will often come to your rescue.

• After a few mistakes and wet patches you will learn how much glue is enough. Most wet patches disappear during the drying process.

*Place the pieces of fabric on the background material and move them around until you are satisfied. At this stage it is still easy to make changes.*

• Do not under any circumstances iron fabric once it has been pasted. It can stretch, and when the fabric cools it will form bubbles.

**13.** *While the background is drying you can carry on cutting out your fabric shapes according to the paper templates.*

**14.** *Each paper pattern will have Pritt Tak on the back. Press the pattern lightly against the fabric you have selected. Using a pair of needlework scissors, cut out the hills, house, roof, tree, washing, windows and doors.*

**15.** *Be careful when taking the paper templates off the fabric that you do not make the fabric fray.*

**16.** *Arrange the cut-out shapes on the background fabric. Move the tree and the house around until they look right. Use your original sketch, but adapt your design according to what the fabric requires. Use two toothpicks with a tiny bit of Pritt Tak on the ends: in this way you can easily pick up and move around even the smallest piece of fabric. But do not glue anything yet.*

**17.** *Now comes the most important step:*
☐ Look at your picture carefully.
☐ Hold it up a little and look at it.
☐ Stand on a chair and look at your picture from above, or hold it up in front of a mirror.
☐ Be critical of the following:
   • Do the colours go well together?
   • Does the picture lack balance?
   • Do any of the pieces of fabric attract too much attention?
   • Try other pieces of fabric in places where something does not look right.

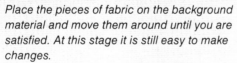

☐ Hold your frame over the picture to see whether the picture fits comfortably in the frame. Move the pieces of fabric slightly inwards if it looks as though the detail is disappearing behind the frame.

☐ Be flexible. This is where the fascination of fabric collage lies. Even at this stage you can change your picture before it is glued.

☐ Let the picture rest for a while. Have a look at it every now and then. The comments of friends and family can be helpful, but trust your instinct and good taste.

☐ Once you are satisfied with the total impression, you can begin gluing.

## THE GLUING PROCESS

*1. Push the point of a pencil slightly under the house and draw very lightly the outlines of the roof and walls onto the background fabric. Do the same with the tree and the hills.*

*2. Now remove all the loose pieces of fabric from the background fabric.*

*3. Spread glue evenly over the whole of the area where you are going to place the hills.*

*4. Now start gluing the hills from the back to the front, in other words, from light to dark. Each piece should slightly overlap the one behind it.*

*5. Spread glue on the background fabric*

*Using a pencil, trace the outlines of the forms very lightly on the background material.*

*First paste down the hills from the back to the front, allowing each to overlap the one behind.*

between the pencil lines you have drawn of the tree and the house and glue these.

**6.** You can now start cutting out and gluing down the finer details.

☐ Cut out and paste the leaves of the tree.

☐ Cut out the windows and the door.
☐ The windows and the door each have two pieces – a dark piece for the frame and a lighter piece for the glass.
☐ The door is cut in long strips for a more interesting texture.
☐ Cut out and glue down the washing line and the clothes, as well as the doorstep.

**7.** *Make the washing line with thread in the following way:*

☐ Cut the thread to the desired length.
☐ Hold the thread in one hand.
☐ Dip the index finger of the other hand into some glue, dab it against your thumb and pull the thread between the thumb and index finger.
☐ Wipe your hands and glue the thread.
☐ Outline the windows and the door with thread and see what a difference it makes.

**8.** *Once each piece of fabric has been stuck down, stand your picture upright or hang it on the wall. Enjoy your big moment and experience the satisfaction of having created something!*

**9.** *There is still time to make changes, but be careful not to fill in bare areas indiscriminately.*

**10.** *Place the frame without glass over the picture and decide whether you are satisfied with the effect.*

The other fabric shapes are then pasted in position. Paste the last details such as the window-panes and washing-line, and there's your picture.

*Example 2:* In this variation bright primary colours are used, and this makes the picture perfectly suited for hanging in a children's room.

**Example 3:** *The plain pastel fabric simply calls out for a few changes to be made to the original design. A design is often influenced by the fabric one intends using.*

**Example 4:** *The same basic pattern is used, but the picture is adapted so as to place more emphasis on the foreground material.*

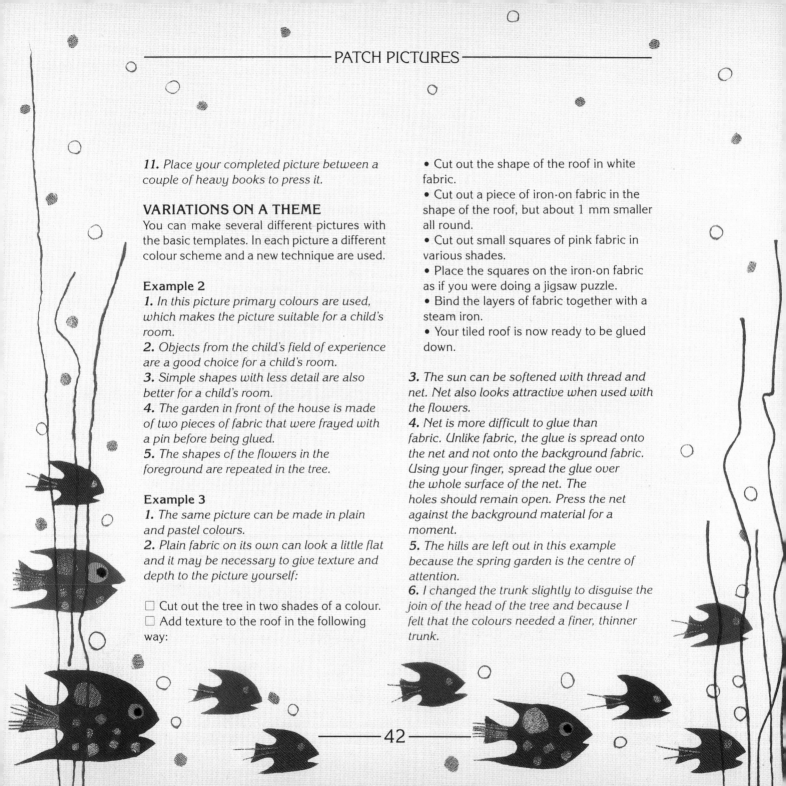

**11.** Place your completed picture between a couple of heavy books to press it.

## VARIATIONS ON A THEME

You can make several different pictures with the basic templates. In each picture a different colour scheme and a new technique are used.

### Example 2

**1.** In this picture primary colours are used, which makes the picture suitable for a child's room.
**2.** Objects from the child's field of experience are a good choice for a child's room.
**3.** Simple shapes with less detail are also better for a child's room.
**4.** The garden in front of the house is made of two pieces of fabric that were frayed with a pin before being glued.
**5.** The shapes of the flowers in the foreground are repeated in the tree.

### Example 3

**1.** The same picture can be made in plain and pastel colours.
**2.** Plain fabric on its own can look a little flat and it may be necessary to give texture and depth to the picture yourself:

☐ Cut out the tree in two shades of a colour.
☐ Add texture to the roof in the following way:

• Cut out the shape of the roof in white fabric.
• Cut out a piece of iron-on fabric in the shape of the roof, but about 1 mm smaller all round.
• Cut out small squares of pink fabric in various shades.
• Place the squares on the iron-on fabric as if you were doing a jigsaw puzzle.
• Bind the layers of fabric together with a steam iron.
• Your tiled roof is now ready to be glued down.

**3.** The sun can be softened with thread and net. Net also looks attractive when used with the flowers.
**4.** Net is more difficult to glue than fabric. Unlike fabric, the glue is spread onto the net and not onto the background fabric. Using your finger, spread the glue over the whole surface of the net. The holes should remain open. Press the net against the background material for a moment.
**5.** The hills are left out in this example because the spring garden is the centre of attention.
**6.** I changed the trunk slightly to disguise the join of the head of the tree and because I felt that the colours needed a finer, thinner trunk.

### Example 4

*1. In this picture the emphasis is on the colour of the fabric in the foreground. Select and arrange colours that sparkle when they are placed next to one another. In the right quantity two complementary colours will sparkle. Unravel or fray the fabric with a pin for an interesting effect.*

*2. The "levels" in the foreground that have been created by the use of colour deserve more attention. I therefore made the house much smaller and placed it in the background. In fact, the house could also be left out completely.*

*3. The tree was too "flat" for the atmosphere of the picture as a whole. Using tacking stitches, I added texture to the trunk before gluing it down. I also frayed the leaves before gluing them down.*

*4. If you have a basic knowledge of embroidery stitches you can add texture to a fabric collage. If you can "paint" creatively with your sewing machine, you can add interest to your picture in this way, too.*

### THE FRAMING OF PICTURES

Your choice of frame will be determined by your choice of subject and the colours of your fabric — they should always go well together. Most department stores stock ready-made frames. If you cannot find what you are looking for there, ask a framer to make you a frame. It is, however, cheaper to frame your picture yourself. This is how you do it:

*1. Place the frame face down.*

*2. With a pair of pliers remove the small nails that hold the glass in position.*

*3. Take out the glass and clean it well.*

*4. Look at your completed picture more closely. Remove all dust and loose threads with a paintbrush or pick them up with a piece of Pritt Tak.*

*5. Place your picture in the frame and behind it place the backing cardboard that usually comes with the frame.*

*6. Turn the picture around carefully while holding the picture and the glass in position with your fingers.*

*7. Make quite sure you have removed every bit of dust. You can be sure you will have to repeat the process a number of times!*

*8. Place the frame face down again and press the small nails against the cardboard in the frame.*

*9. Cut out a piece of brown paper to exactly the same size as the back of the frame.*

*10. Spread wood and paper glue over the back of the frame and paste the brown paper over it.*

*11. Attach hooks about one-third of the way down the back of the frame. Tie a strong piece of string between the two hooks, and your picture is ready to be hung.*

# CHAPTER 5

# *Every picture tells a story*

The inspiration for a picture could come from anywhere. To illustrate this, here are the stories behind some of my pictures.

## Peaceful Kingdom

This picture was made for a Christmas display. I initially intended the picture to be for a child's room and I was going to fill the Peaceful Kingdom with well-known animals. The fabric I chose was a blue ethnic print. I realised very soon that my choice of fabric was not suitable for the kind of animals I had had in mind. I had to change either the fabric or the animals. After thinking about it for a few days I allowed myself to be guided by the fabric, and cut out more abstract ethnic shapes.

I hardly ever use designs in the fabric to suggest something such as a flower or an animal, but in this case it happened quite by chance. I was cutting out the fabric around the sun, which happened to fall onto my work. My family saw this and felt that it was the perfect sun. After this, the picture took its course and I cut out flowers, grass, insects and the ground from the design of the fabric.

This blue printed fabric is ideal to use to start gluing with, because you can use glue quite liberally without its showing through. The only disadvantage of the fabric is that it shrinks slightly when it dries.

## A present for the first day

This picture was inspired by the English song that goes:
"On the first day of Christmas my true love
    sent to me . . .
A partridge in a pear tree . . ."
This to me is still the most charming gift anyone could receive – your own partridge in a pear tree!

Of course, initially, there would have been only one partridge but wherever I placed the partridge in the tree, it did not feel right. Only when I made a mate for it did I feel satisfied with the effect. Using gold thread and simple embroidery stitches, I added more sparkle and texture to the birds.

## "The earth laughs in flowers"

These pictures were made in the spring of 1987 and were inspired by the quotation: "The earth laughs in flowers".

Often when I read a poem, a rhyme or a beautiful quotation, a kind of story begins to unfold in my thoughts. It was, in fact, spring when I read this quotation. The whole world was in bloom and the exuberance of the colours so inspired me that I wanted to make pictures in which laughing flowers took over and ruled the world.

The predominant colour in my thoughts was green, because no green is as beautiful as the green of springtime. The flowers had to look as though they were growing and I wanted to emphasise the idea of growth further with the vertical stripes of the hills. The striped hills were made from strips of fabric placed next to one another and joined onto a white background with iron-on fabric. The hills were then cut out and pasted in position. Black was used as a contrast in order to give the colours of the flowers extra sparkle.

*"Peaceful Kingdom"* appears on page 44.
**Left:** *"A Present for the First Day".*
**Below and right:** *"The Earth Laughs in Flowers".*

# CHAPTER 6

## Fabric artists and their work

In this chapter a few fabric artists share their work with you. Their work is inspiring and a sheer pleasure to view. It gives you the assurance that everyone, within the framework of his or her own interests, ability and skills, can experiment with fabric. If a piece of material can be sewn, it can be glued, and if it can be glued, it can be sewn. Each artist in this chapter has her own approach and technique, and her own colour, fabric and design preferences. Some prefer to work with glue, and others prefer to "paint" with needle and thread. However, they all have one thing in common − a love of fabric and the fabric collages one can make with it. Examples of their work are included to show different approaches to fabric collage, and to provide a variety of examples as inspiration.

Jeannie Walker has an inspiring philosophy: "There is room for all in fabric art, for the timid and the adventurous, old and young, male and female. It is not necessary to use hand stitching; similar effects can be achieved on the sewing machine. Instead of using stitches to make a design, effects can also be created entirely by fabric manipulation to gain wonderful results."

**Above:** *A collage in suede by Jeannie Walker.*
**Left:** *"Fireworks" by Jeannie Walker.*

## JEANNIE WALKER

Jeannie Walker is an artist in the true sense of the word − someone with a special feeling for textiles, colour and texture. She obtained her Fine Arts degree and specialised in book illustration. As a result of an allergy to paint thinner, Jeannie had to give up oil painting. Although fabric art was initially an easier substitute, Jeannie investigated the potential of this medium so thoroughly that she is doing pioneering work in an unusual art form.

As a child she was very interested in embroidery and was encouraged by her talented mother. The approach at that time was still traditional, but it formed the basis for Jeannie's later studies in creative textiles. Jeannie's interest in fabric art was also stimulated by the patchwork craze of the Seventies. Even then her approach was entirely individual. While everyone was doing appliqué work with floral fabric, which was fashionable at the time, she was making patchwork cushions using the luxury fabric of men's ties.

In 1985 Jeannie spent a year studying at the Loughborough College of Art and Design, Leicestershire, England. She did a course in design and embroidery. Most of the students tackled this course with a traditional knowledge of embroidery. The course itself was directed towards experimentation; students were continually reminded that all preconceived ideas and rules were there to be broken and that a re-investigation was necessary. They were therefore given the opportunity to experiment with a wide variety of materials such as fabric, plastic, metal, porcelain and thread.

Today Jeannie does creative "rough" embroidery with rich, luxurious fabrics such as organza, viscose, silk and satin. She complements, contrasts or accentuates these fabrics with a variety of metallic threads. She manipulates the fabric; she crumples, folds, rolls and pads it. She uses iron-on fabric and conjures with "disappearing" fabric and metallic thread.

Jeannie's use of colour is warm and ingenious. She strives for that fascinating quality of colours that vibrate and react to one another. She works in bright plain colours and shades of them, with a few contrasting shadow colours and tints. For her, if the colours do not go well together, more work must be done.

To be able to share your knowledge is in itself an art. Jeannie has a unique gift in that her presence gives her students the self-confidence to experiment. Her approach is never prescriptive, critical or derogatory. She encourages and acknowledges individuality. She recommends that you should always be on the lookout for new ideas. Make copies of everything that inspires you, be it pottery, glassware, beautiful baskets, jewellery or appliqué work. You will often find ideas for colour combinations in fashion magazines.

Jeannie admits that her inspiration does not come in a flash of insight, but that it develops over a period of time. It is for this reason that she finds fabric art so fascinating. During this germination period she can give further thought to her design. Fabric and colours can be added or removed and "mistakes" rectified.

At present she is working on a book on creative stitchery in which one of her aims is to share her unique feeling for colour with the reader.

*Jeannie Walker's use of colour is striking.*

## KAFFIE PRETORIUS

Kaffie Pretorius deserves a place of honour in this book because she is what you could call a pioneer of fabric art. In the Seventies Kaffie was largely responsible for the resurgence of interest in fabric art. During her stay in the United States of America she came into contact with fabric art, and on her return home she taught fabric work for several years, even though she had no formal art training. Today Kaffie paints full-time, but she admits that time and again she returns to working with fabric, just for the feel of it and because fabric work and painting complement each other so well. Kaffie exploits the full potential of fabric. She uses quilting or fabric together with paint in her paintings. When she combines fabric work and embroidery, her cushions are small fabric paintings. Kaffie makes Christmas presents for her friends out of fabric: handy articles for everyday use, which she finishes off on a personal note with her own fabric label. A high point of Kaffie's pioneering work was the children's book that she illustrated with a series of twelve fabric pictures.

Kaffie is an "olde worlde" person. She likes old fabric and seldom buys new fabric. Her fabric collection comes from far and wide: she gets old, used fabrics from various local people, and soft, fine floral fabrics from friends in America. She likes cutting up old clothes and is the proud owner of a bag full of silk ties from someone with exceptional taste.

If you were to ask Kaffie what colours she likes working with, she would reply immediately: earth colours — strong, warm colours that reflect a bond with the land. Kaffie likes to depict simple, honest things in her fabric work, and she is inspired by sea birds, fish, buck and flowers; themes close to her heart.

"Illusion of Freedom" was inspired by a poem Kaffie read. In flight the seagull looks free, but it is only an illusion, because there is no such thing as freedom. Here Kaffie uses fabric of different textures in the natural colours ivory and cream, symbolising the beauty of the bird.

*"Illusion of Freedom." Kaffie Pretorius tries to convey the feeling of the country in her work.*

## CAROL MANGIAGALLI

Carol grew up in Zambia and from an early age was encouraged by her mother to draw and paint. After studying Fine Art she worked as a textile designer. Carol likes decorating things: she likes decorating her house, paints wooden furniture and trays, and also likes painting on glass. She also does pen and ink sketches. Carol has a particular liking for fabric. After initially doing patchwork and quilting, in 1978 she began gluing off-cuts because the process was quicker than sewing. She so enjoyed this method of working with fabric that since then she has already had five exhibitions. She finds fabric a soft medium and, with the variety of textures, colours and patterns available, it always offers new challenges. Although Carol prefers natural fabrics such as cotton, linen, silk and lace, she also uses synthetic fabric, according to what she needs for her picture. She likes working with a variety of colours – from bright to soft pastels. She has had a number of exhibitions, including a one-man exhibition of her work.

Carol prefers a rural life style. The time she spent in the rural areas of Ireland, the architecture of old buildings, old furniture and the colours of the landscape have had a great influence on her work. Beautiful things, the environment and humour inspire Carol. She enjoys doing still-life works, landscapes, pictures with flowers and buildings, and domestic scenes with furniture, cats, dogs and birds. She also does humorous portraits of her friends. Carol enjoys her creativity, and creates a happy atmosphere in her pictures.

*Carol Mangiagalli's view of her home town.*

## KITTY PETOUSIS

Kitty Petousis and her husband own a hotel in a building which was built in 1799 as a country residence. The hotel is situated on a river and offers some spectacular mountain views. The hotel exudes a particular atmosphere which inspired Kitty to set about making a collage for every room, and today the hotel boasts 130 such collages. The country atmosphere, which has often served as an inspiration, in addition sets them off to perfection. Kitty talks about her work spontaneously, and her pictures reflect the same spontaneity. "Oh, every picture is a struggle. You know! You sit there with the pile of fabric in front of you and you know you have to get a picture out of it. So what do you do? You just start. You put a piece here and another piece there, oh and then it just looks terrible! Then I 'jazz' it up a bit here and join a bit more there, and eventually it looks like something!"

Kitty comes from an artistic family and took art as a subject at school. She later studied dietetics and worked at the Ministry of Food in London for five years. Despite her busy career in the hotel industry, which takes up most of her time, Kitty is one of those inspiring people who still manages to create extra time in which she can satisfy her creative urges. She is an example to those who suppress their creativity, using the excuse that they cannot find the time because of other commitments.

In Kitty's active life fabric work is her hobby, and she admits that she has to be spurred on to create something new, because she becomes depressed if the same ideas reappear in her work. Kitty started by embroidering "drawings" by hand. She later started to "draw" with her sewing machine and combined this with appliqué. She prefers appliqué because it gives quick results, the technique is so simple, and it is so decorative. She believes that anyone can do it and that you have only to make a *start* to see how easy it really is.

Kitty is thrifty by nature. She works with the fabric she already has and has no colour preferences. The most beautiful pictures Kitty has ever done were made from the fabric of a friend's Indian dress! Kitty works quickly and spontaneously with her machine. She plans according to the way her picture progresses. Her pictures are strikingly simple and radiate warmth.

*One of the many creations by Kitty Petousis that hang in the hotel run by her and her husband.*

## CINDY BARTOS

Cindy studied Graphic Design and it was during this time that she discovered the wonder of fabric. She admits that although she never mastered the sewing machine, her love of fabric, colour and texture led her to seek another form of expression. She found the answer in gluing and manipulating fabric. The world of textiles became Cindy's profession and she is exposed daily to the latest designs and textures. She finds it a pity that sophisticated technology provides ready-made fabrics and that we no longer weave our own.

In her fabric art Cindy prefers to work with old fabric. She has

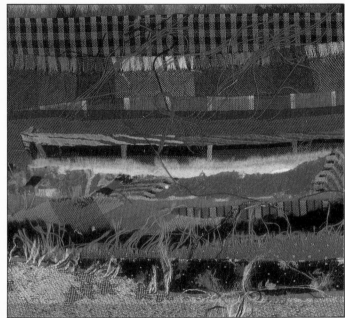

*Cindy Bartos even uses faded denim.*

four enormous jars of off-cuts and she still finds it exciting that time and again she is able to create something new from them. Each picture has its own feeling, is another place, another season or time of day. For Cindy colour and texture are more important than detail. The fine threads and small beads give her abstract landscapes a special effect. If you have a closer look you will notice that it is the clever juxtaposition of certain kinds of fabric and certain colours that creates a feeling of depth and space. She sometimes works with rich, luxurious velvet, and sometimes with lace and small beads. Even frayed and faded denim has a place in her pictures.

Part of the allure of Cindy's pictures lies in their smell. It was when I studied her pictures from close up that their incredible smell overwhelmed me with nostalgia. Cindy's pieces of fabric have the fragrance of very, very old fabric that has been lovingly preserved and cared for over the years in dark attics and old linen chests – a soft, antique fragrance that takes you back in time.

## LESLEY THOMPSON

Lesley Thompson is one of those people who always believed they were not artistic — until she began to glue fabric. For the past few years Lesley has derived endless pleasure from her fabric pictures. After she had initially done patchwork she decided that there had to be a quicker and easier way, and so started experimenting with fabric and glue. Today Lesley has an active home industry and regularly takes part in crafts markets. Because she has small children it has always been important for her to work from home, and in her case fabric pictures were the answer. She supplies department stores and gift shops with a variety of cheerful and colourful pictures for children, and in this way earns herself pocket money.

*Lesley Thompson prefers pictures in bright primary colours — ideal for a children's room.*

Lesley prefers bright primary colours and works mainly in coarse cotton, fine cotton and polycotton. She does pictures for children's rooms: simple pictures with a minimum of detail. She usually depicts well-known themes from the child's field of experience with which he or she can easily identify. Her success with fabric pictures has given Lesley a great deal of confidence in her new-found creativity. She believes that inside each person there is an artist waiting to be discovered.

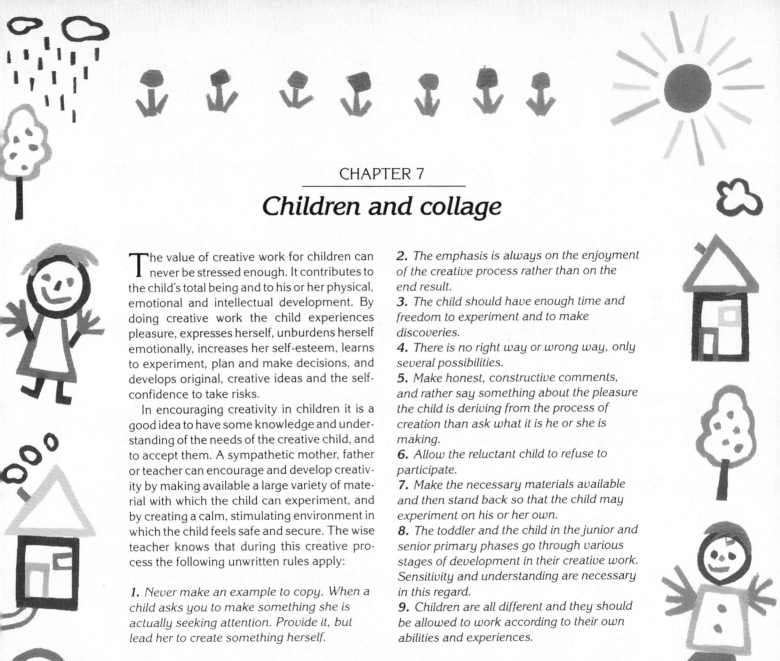

## CHAPTER 7

# *Children and collage*

The value of creative work for children can never be stressed enough. It contributes to the child's total being and to his or her physical, emotional and intellectual development. By doing creative work the child experiences pleasure, expresses herself, unburdens herself emotionally, increases her self-esteem, learns to experiment, plan and make decisions, and develops original, creative ideas and the self-confidence to take risks.

In encouraging creativity in children it is a good idea to have some knowledge and under-standing of the needs of the creative child, and to accept them. A sympathetic mother, father or teacher can encourage and develop creativity by making available a large variety of material with which the child can experiment, and by creating a calm, stimulating environment in which the child feels safe and secure. The wise teacher knows that during this creative process the following unwritten rules apply:

*1. Never make an example to copy. When a child asks you to make something she is actually seeking attention. Provide it, but lead her to create something herself.*

*2. The emphasis is always on the enjoyment of the creative process rather than on the end result.*
*3. The child should have enough time and freedom to experiment and to make discoveries.*
*4. There is no right way or wrong way, only several possibilities.*
*5. Make honest, constructive comments, and rather say something about the pleasure the child is deriving from the process of creation than ask what it is he or she is making.*
*6. Allow the reluctant child to refuse to participate.*
*7. Make the necessary materials available and then stand back so that the child may experiment on his or her own.*
*8. The toddler and the child in the junior and senior primary phases go through various stages of development in their creative work. Sensitivity and understanding are necessary in this regard.*
*9. Children are all different and they should be allowed to work according to their own abilities and experiences.*

## THE VALUE OF FABRIC COLLAGE

*1. Collage offers the opportunity to experiment with a large variety of materials – not only with fabric. The child should be especially encouraged to use fabric together with other media.*

*2. The child develops a feeling for combining and grouping materials and in this way becomes acquainted with elements of design and composition.*

*3. The child learns to think about choices and to make decisions.*

*4. The colour and texture of fabric contribute to the quality of the picture. The colour of fabric is "ready-made" and children learn a great deal about colour by working with fabric.*

*5. Collage offers the opportunity to work together in a group. It contributes to the child's social development. Physically he or she learns to work close to someone else. The child learns to share space, equipment and ideas. Some children derive particular benefit from group work. The less creative and skilful children are encouraged by the more creative children. Some lead and others follow.*

*6. The child feels important, knowing that his or her effort contributes towards the whole.*

*7. Children like to see quick results, and a group collage takes a relatively short time to finish. It is easy to complete a picture before the children's enthusiasm wanes.*

*8. In our society the joy of fabric is sometimes wasted on the male sex. Boys often would not dream of touching a needle and thread, but they are very willing to experiment with fabric, glue and paint.*

## PREPARATION

☐ Decide what materials you are going to provide. Choose a variety that is aesthetically pleasing together.

☐ It is a good idea to use two tables: a table on which to choose fabric, and a work table. Arrange all the materials attractively and invitingly.

☐ Get all the equipment ready: aprons, glue brushes, pairs of scissors, a variety of fabrics, buttons, beads, lace, cord and thread. Also provide paint, wax crayons and pencil crayons.

## INTRODUCTION TO THE ACTIVITY

Your group's ability and experience will to a large extent determine the way you prepare them for a collage activity. The following guidelines may be useful:

☐ The children should be encouraged to experience their surroundings with all their senses.

☐ Outings and shared experiences broaden a child's horizon. Children should also be encouraged to take a fresh look at familiar surroundings and to observe small details.

☐ Discuss the following aspects:

• Colours and shades.
• Texture. Allow children to rub and stroke, and to talk about the way surfaces feel.
• Talk about fabric. It can be soft or firm, floral, striped or plain, and it can be crumpled, folded, torn or frayed.
• Encourage children to think about their choice of fabric and about how they are going to combine it with other media.

## A PRACTICAL EXAMPLE

Francine Nepgen's art school is situated in idyllic surroundings. The beautiful gardens, the giant oaks and the dignity of the historic building combine to create a restful yet stimulating atmosphere in which little artists with paint-stained overalls can experiment to their heart's content.

At this art school the children become acquainted with a wide variety of media. They investigate all the possibilities of crayon and brush, work with potter's clay, make models with wire netting and papier-mâché, make and clothe wooden figures, and do fabric collage. In one corner of Francine's classroom is a red washbasket full of pieces of fabric. Bright and multi-coloured fabric protrudes from each opening. On top of this pile are the remnants of a jersey that was never completed. It is gloriously coloured in yellow, purple and pink. On the wall there is a bird wearing a sock that was cut out of this same knitting — creative ideas!

**Above:** *A group collage by the senior group of a nursery school.*
**Overleaf:** *In her picture Zonja Nel expresses her sorrow at the practice of allowing very young chickens to brood.*

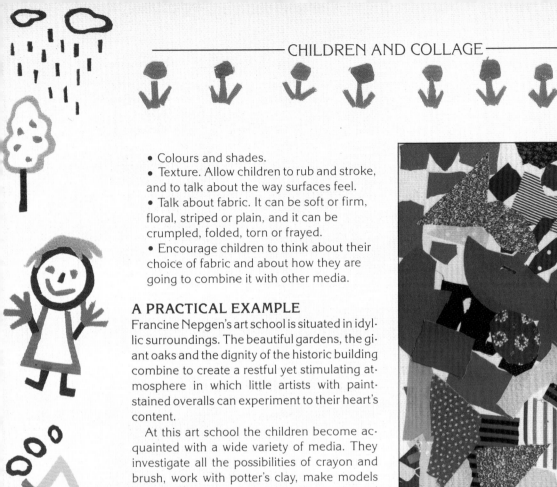

*Barry*

*Cezanne*

*Samantha*

## FABRIC COLLAGE FOR THE JUNIOR GROUP

For the junior group Francine presented a bird theme, "Strange birds that we do not know". The lack of limits in the theme was so that the children would not be afraid to take risks.

The point with youngsters is that they do not yet use materials that aid the painting process. They "paint" as it were with the materials to "clothe" their birds, and the background is then painted around the birds.

As an introduction Francine and her group discussed birds. The children were encouraged to share what they knew about birds with one another. They were led from the known to the unknown. They discussed the shapes, sizes and colours of birds. They shared their knowledge on wings, feathers, claws and beaks. They looked at and felt a variety of feathers. Francine also encouraged them to change into birds so that they could physically experience the way a bird sits, stands, sleeps, takes off, flies and lands. By the end of the discussion the children

were so inspired they could hardly wait to start working. Francine believes that you should close the discussion at this point and that when the children first start to be creative, it is preferable not to add anything further. Children like to please adults and a comment at this stage on, for example, beaks may lead to everybody starting to think alike and all the beaks looking the same.

The youngsters were encouraged to examine the fabric and to think about the texture of the bird and what it would feel like to touch it. They were also encouraged to use paint to repeat in the background the colour and texture of the fabric. Another principle that was conveyed to the children is that darker paint and fabric next to the body of the bird can create an impression of movement and depth.

Barry's ostrich moves in black and white. Wynand's swallow has satin wings. The area closest to the body of the bird is black, whereas for the outer area he has used a lighter, bottle-green

Susannah

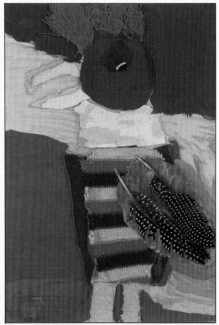

Simone

Margo

Peter

Wynand

satin. Wynand and Peter's birds soar because of the clever repetition of blue and green in the background.

Carla's duck is luxuriously decked out in bottle-green satin and wine-red velvet. The texture of the fabric enabled her to portray most effectively what she knows about ducks. The changing colour, sparkle and sheen of velvet and satin make these materials excellent choices to represent the texture of a duck's plumage.

Susannah's bird is given movement because the foremost wing is made of a coarser, darker fabric. The light yellow wing at the back almost moves backwards. Under the wing in front she has repeated some of the floral designs in the fabric in crayon and paint. In her picture Samantha also repeats the floral designs in the fabric in shades of pink.

Cezanne's king of birds rules with outstretched, striped wings. There is a piece of fabric on the breast striped in blue, purple, pink and black. These stripes and colours are repeated in the wings with fabric and wool. Simone's striped bird is attired in velvet, curtain fabric, wool and towelling. With its rich texture and genuine feathers it asks to be touched. A facial expression often determines a bird's character. Margo's bird stands proudly upright, despite the evident sleepiness.

*Carla*

*Tamara and the bird with the coloured sock.*

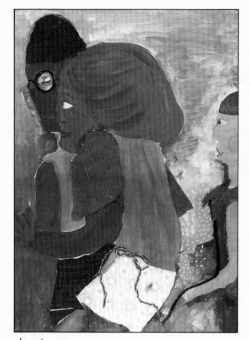

Janet

Sarah

Gabby

## FABRIC COLLAGE FOR THE SENIOR GROUP

With the older child, collage is a question of adding a variety of materials in order to develop painting. The older child is encouraged to make fabric a part of her painting; in other words, the transition from fabric to paint should be a subtle one. There should also be a repetition of colour and texture to make the eye move. With printed fabric the child can have a large variety of textures in her picture.

The theme Francine presented to the older children was: "I am running away to hide". This is an original theme with plenty of potential for movement, colour and texture. During the preparation the children actually did run and hide. They took turns to be models while the others watched carefully. Questions such as the following were examined: How does a person move if she is going to hide — quickly, in a crouch, carefully, fearfully, quietly or on tiptoe? What do a person's hands, legs, feet and back look like when she runs? What do a person's clothes look like?

Helen

*Elton*

*Margaret*

Francine also did figure studies with the children and looked at the proportions of various parts of the body. What the children experienced is reflected in their pictures.

Janet's little girl is running carefully, shoulders pulled up in a beautiful hiding-away movement.

In Margaret's picture there is a great deal of movement and life. She earnestly assures Francine that her people really exist, and her use of loose, folded fabric gives her picture an added dimension.

In Sarah's picture there is a strong repetition of colour in the blue checked fabric. Helen "frames" her picture with a repetition of the dots.

Gabby repeats the black and white pattern of the fabric so that your glance moves over the picture.

Elton's transition from fabric to paint was very subtly done and it is not easy to see where the black and white-spotted fabric ends and the paint begins. The pleats in the dress are very well done and are a very good example of manipulated fabric.

Francine encourages her pupils to think of themselves as artists, and her own paint-smeared overall reassures them that they are there to experiment with abandon and that it is fine if their artists' overalls get dirty, and remain unwashed!

*Some simple designs for a children's room.*

# CHAPTER 8

# Conclusion: a few thoughts and ideas

There is some measure of creativity in everyone. Believe in it and use it regularly. Only by persevering and practising will you grow and develop your own style. Believe in yourself and in your taste, work to please yourself, and never let criticism discourage you. You are an artist in your own right. Do not feel intimidated by someone whose work is better than yours. Rather regard his or her work as inspiration.

No one is perfect. Tradition "obliged" early fabric artists to make a mistake in every piece of work they did so as not to compete with the Creator. Be proud of your work and sign it. See fabric collage as a voyage of discovery. Try to enjoy the journey just as much as the arrival.

You can make fabric pictures for pleasure or for profit. Once you have enough pictures for your own collection and have made a picture for each of your fabric donors, you could perhaps start thinking about selling some of your pictures. Craft work is an honourable way of earning money. Fabric pictures are charming and are a very popular item at craft markets. This kind of market is becoming increasingly popular and most large cities and towns already boast a unique gathering place of this type for those engaged in arts and crafts, who inspire one another.

You could perhaps join a market like this because you would then work more regularly and purposefully and in this way improve your feeling for fabric, design, colour and technique. With the money you earn from this, you could buy yourself some new fabric.

Use this book as a starting point. Feel free to copy till you have mastered the technique of collage, but after that follow your own initiative and ideas. You will derive far more satisfaction from your own original work.

The following pages will give you an insight into the thought processes involved when making a fabric picture. Usually each picture starts off with a visual impression of something concrete or realistic. Included are a number of sketches of such visual impressions – these are usually placed on file. When you want to make a fabric picture of some such object, it is a good idea to make another sketch, this time more simplified, practical and workable in fabric. You will also notice how the final result in fabric depicts only the essentials.

*While on an outing, take photographs or make sketches. Try to remember what it was that struck you the most, and portray only the essence. Collage demands a simplification which is possible only if you express your feelings.*

*Do not be afraid of using people in your pictures – people make pictures less lonely. Look at the way people sit, stand, move, fight, gossip or sleep. Think about the spontaneous naïve figures children love to draw.*

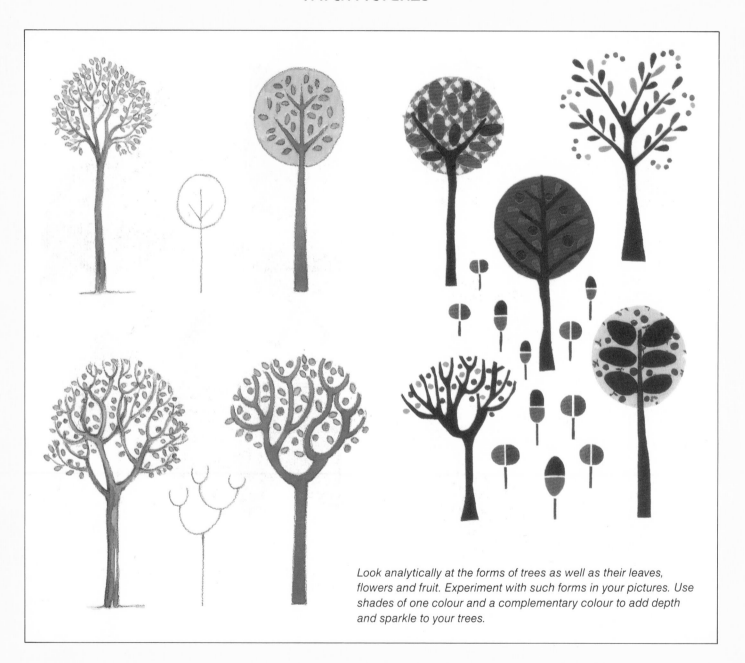

*Look analytically at the forms of trees as well as their leaves, flowers and fruit. Experiment with such forms in your pictures. Use shades of one colour and a complementary colour to add depth and sparkle to your trees.*

Some ideas for making fabric birds. The character of each bird is determined to a great extent by the expression in the eyes. Move the cut out eyes around and try various possibilities before you paste them down.

# Bibliography

Alexander, E.: *Fabric Pictures*, Mills & Boon, London, 1959
Ashurst, E.: *Collage*, Marshall Cavendish, London, 1976
Brown, E.: *Creative Quilting*, Pitman, London, 1975
Coleman, A.: *The Creative Sewing Machine*, Batsford, London, 1979
Connor, M.: *Introducing Fabric Collage*, Batsford, London, 1969
French, B.: *Principles of Collage*, Mills & Boon, London, 1969
Healey, D.: *Living with Colour*, Macmillan, London, 1982
Itten, J.: *The Art of Colour*, Otto Maier, Ravensburg, 1973
Kay, F.: *Starting Fabric Collage*, Studio Vista, London, 1969
Rushton, D.: *Collages*, Pelham Books, London, 1984
Schäpper, L.: *A Modern Approach to Patchwork*, Batsford, London, 1984
Scrase, P.: *Let's Start Designing*, Studio Vista, London, 1966
Solvit, M.-J.: *Pictures in Patchwork*, Oak Tree Press, London, 1977
Walker, M.: *Quiltmaking in Patchwork and Applique*, Ebury Press, London, 1985

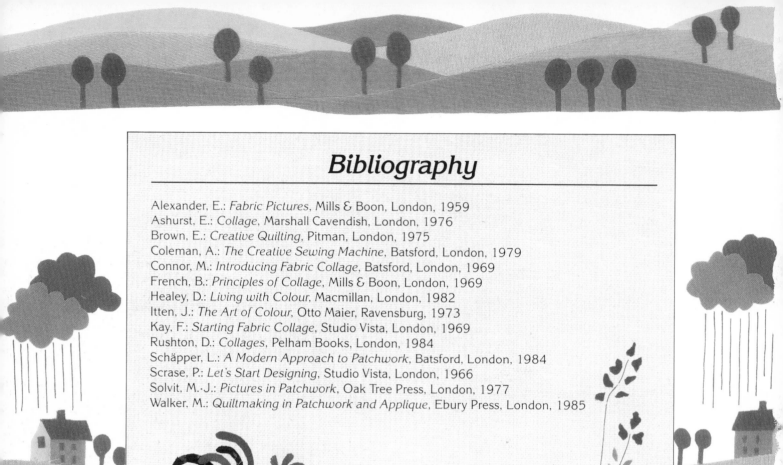